ALY RAISM
The Gymnast Who Never Gave Up
Jim G. Britto

SHE WAS BORN ON MAY 25, 1994, IN A TOWN CALLED NEEDHAM, MASSACHUSETTS

Ever heard of Aly Raisman? She's not just any ordinary person—Aly is like a real-life superhero of the gymnastics world! She flips, flies, and twirls through the air, just like a bird, only with even more sparkle

Her mom even says Aly couldn't stop flipping and jumping—she always seemed to be upside down!

Who Should Read This Book

This book about Aly Raisman is perfect for a wide range of readers, including:

Young Gymnasts: Children interested in gymnastics will find inspiration in Aly's journey, learning about the dedication and hard work needed to succeed in the sport.

Sports Enthusiasts: Kids who love sports in general can appreciate Aly's story, as it highlights themes of teamwork, perseverance, and goal-setting.

Aly Raisman Fans: Anyone who admires Aly's achievements, courage, and advocacy will enjoy learning more about her life and impact on gymnastics and beyond.

Students Learning About Role Models: Teachers can use this book in classrooms to discuss important qualities like leadership, resilience, and speaking out for what is right, encouraging kids to follow their dreams.

Parents and Guardians: Adults looking for inspirational stories to share with their children can use Aly's journey as a motivational tool, showing the importance of believing in oneself and standing up for others.

Kids Ages 7-13: The book is tailored specifically for this age group, making it engaging and accessible for young readers.

Anyone Interested in Overcoming Challenges: Readers of all ages can find inspiration in Aly's ability to face and overcome obstacles, whether in sports or life.

TABLE CONTENT

The Wobbly Beginnings of Gymnastics

A long, long time ago (we're talking thousands of years!), people didn't have trampolines or fancy mats to flip on. But guess what? They still loved to jump, roll, and twist! Gymnastics began as a fun way for humans to move their bodies and, sometimes, just show off a little.

It All Started with… Soldiers?!

Way back in Ancient Greece, soldiers were told, "If you want to be a warrior, you need to train your body like one!" So they practiced running, jumping, climbing, and doing flips (which were probably wobbly at first!). They thought, "If we can do this, we can win battles!"

They even had something called the "Pentathlon"—where they threw things like javelins, jumped over stuff, and wrestled. Imagine a soldier in the air trying to do a cartwheel! (We bet they laughed a lot at first!)

Roman Gymnastics – From Fighting to Fun!

The Romans loved copying the Greeks, but they wanted to have even more fun. They built big arenas and showed off their moves! They balanced on horses, jumped through hoops, and tumbled for the crowds. It wasn't just for soldiers anymore—now everyone thought gymnastics looked cool.

One Roman kid probably said, "Look, Mom, I can somersault like a pro!" (And then landed on their head—oops!)

Oops, Gymnastics Went Missing!

For a long time, gymnastics kind of disappeared when knights and castles became the big thing in Europe. People were too busy with swords and dragons to practice backflips!

The Comeback: Hello, Modern Gymnastics!

Fast forward to about 200 years ago in Germany, a man named Friedrich Jahn decided, "We need gymnastics back!" He built the first gym (no, not the kind with treadmills) with cool equipment like bars, rings, and beams. Kids started swinging, flipping, and balancing—and gymnastics was back in action!

Gymnastics Goes Global!

Soon, other countries joined the fun, and gymnastics became so popular it became an Olympic sport in 1896! Since then, people from all over the world have competed to see who can do the coolest tricks without falling on their noses.

Gymnastics Today – Fun for Everyone!

Today, gymnastics isn't just for warriors or knights—it's for anyone who loves to move! Whether you're doing a cartwheel in your backyard or watching gymnasts twist in the air at the Olympics, gymnastics is all about having fun, working hard, and never giving up (even if you land on your butt sometimes)!

And that's how gymnastics went from wobbly soldiers to the awesome flips and tricks we see today! Keep practicing—you never know, you might just land your first perfect cartwheel!

CHAPTER 1: Who is Aly Raisman?

Hey there, future gymnast! Ever heard of Aly Raisman? She's not just any ordinary person—Aly is like a real-life superhero of the gymnastics world! She flips, flies, and twirls through the air, just like a bird, only with even more sparkle! Let's dive into her fun and inspiring story.

Aly as a Little Kid

Before Aly was an Olympic champion, she was just a little girl with big dreams. She was born on May 25, 1994, in a town called Needham, Massachusetts. Little Aly loved dancing around the house, climbing on furniture (oops!), and doing cartwheels on the grass. Her mom even says Aly couldn't stop flipping and jumping—she always seemed to be upside down!

One day, Aly told her parents, "I want to be a gymnast!" Her mom probably laughed and thought, "Let's see if she means it." Spoiler alert: She DID!

When Practice Becomes Play

Aly started going to gymnastics classes when she was just a kid. It wasn't easy at first. She'd fall off the balance beam (a LOT!), land on her butt during somersaults, and sometimes just tumble into giggles.

But Aly had a superpower—she never gave up! She practiced every day, getting better with each flip. Some days were hard, and some days were fun, but Aly kept saying to herself: "One day, I'll make it to the Olympics!"

The Olympics Dream Comes True!

When Aly was 18 years old, her dream finally came true—she made it to the 2012 Olympics in London! Can you imagine wearing a sparkly Team USA outfit and performing in front of the whole world? It was super nerve-wracking, but Aly stayed cool.

She dazzled the crowd with her flips, leaps, and perfect landings. Guess what? Aly won two gold medals and one bronze! She was now one of the best gymnasts in the world! After her big wins, people started calling her "Captain Aly" because she was the leader of the team.

Aly's Big Comeback

But Aly wasn't done yet! Four years later, she returned to the Olympics in Rio in 2016. Many people thought she might be too old to compete—can you believe that? But Aly didn't listen to them. She trained harder than ever and showed the world that age is just a number.

In Rio, she won another two silver medals and one gold medal! Talk about an incredible comeback.

Aly's Courage Outside the Gym

Aly isn't just amazing on the gymnastics mat—she's also a hero in real life. After the Olympics, Aly spoke up about some really important things. She wanted to make sure that all athletes feel safe and respected. She stood up for what was right, showing the world that being brave means more than just doing flips—it also means speaking up when something is wrong.

What is Aly Doing Today?

Today, Aly is still inspiring people, even though she's not competing anymore. She spends her time helping kids, encouraging others to chase their dreams, and showing everyone the importance of being kind. Aly loves talking about mental health and self-care—that means taking care of your body and your mind!

She also works with lots of organizations to help others. And guess what? She still loves doing gymnastics for fun. Once a gymnast, always a gymnast!

What We Can Learn from Aly

Aly's story teaches us that:
It's okay to fall as long as you get back up.
Dreams can come true if you work hard and believe in yourself.
Being brave doesn't just mean being strong on the outside—it means standing up for what's right.
So, what do you think? Do you feel like doing a cartwheel or two right now? Just like Aly, you can achieve anything if you put in the effort, have fun, and never give up. Who knows? Maybe one day, we'll be cheering for you at the Olympics!
Now flip, twist, and keep dreaming big!

Fun Facts About Aly Raisman's Childhood

1. Flipping All Over the House

Aly's parents say she was always flipping, rolling, and jumping around the house—even on the couch and bed! She couldn't stay still for long. (We bet she kept her parents on their toes!)

2. Dancing Queen!

Before Aly became a gymnast, she loved to dance around the living room. Her favorite music? The songs from her mom's old gymnastics tapes! She even did little routines for her family.

3. First Gymnastics Class at 2 Years Old

Aly started gymnastics at the age of 2—yes, TWO! She probably couldn't even say "cartwheel" properly yet but was already trying to do one!

4. Sports Lover

Even though Aly loved gymnastics the most, she also tried other sports like soccer and ice skating. But she always found her way back to gymnastics—because flying through the air was way more fun!

5. Favorite Snack: Peanut Butter & Jelly Sandwiches

When Aly came home from practice, she loved munching on a PB&J sandwich. It gave her the energy to keep doing flips all day long!

6. A Bit Shy, but Very Determined

Little Aly was a bit shy around new people, but once she stepped onto the gymnastics floor, she became super brave. It was like she had a secret switch that turned her into a superstar!

7. Loved Watching Gymnastics on TV

Aly's biggest inspiration was the 2004 Olympic gymnastics team. She watched their routines over and over, dreaming of being just like them someday. (And guess what? She made her dream come true!)

8. A Big Sister with Big Hugs

Aly is the oldest of four siblings, which means she was like the "boss" of the house. But instead of being bossy, she gave lots of hugs and tried to inspire her younger siblings. (We wonder if they tried copying her flips too!)

9. Backyard Gymnastics Fun

Aly used to practice doing handstands and cartwheels in the backyard. Sometimes she fell into the grass, laughed it off, and tried again. She made gymnastics look easy—and fun!

10. Always a Good Sport

Even as a kid, Aly believed in being kind and respectful to her teammates. If she didn't win, she'd clap for the other kids and try harder next time. That's why everyone liked her—she had a heart as big as her dreams!

These fun facts show that Aly was just like any other kid—full of energy, curiosity, and determination. With hard work and lots of fun along the way, she became a superstar gymnast!

Now, who's ready to do some flips?

CHAPTER 2: Twirling into Gymnastics

How Aly Fell in Love with Gymnastics

Aly Raisman's love for gymnastics started when she was just a little girl, and it's a fun story filled with flips, sparkles, and lots of practice!

It All Started with a TV Show

One day, when Aly was around 6 years old, she sat on the couch with her family, watching the 2004 Olympics on TV. As soon as she saw the gymnasts flipping, jumping, and flying through the air, her eyes got HUGE.

She said to herself, "I want to do THAT!" The sparkly leotards, the twists, the cheering crowd—it was like magic. Aly didn't just watch the show; she felt it in her heart. She wanted to be like those gymnasts, standing tall on the podium with a gold medal.

First Gymnastics Class: A Little Nervous but Super Excited

After watching the Olympics, Aly begged her parents to sign her up for gymnastics classes. When she finally walked into the gym for her first lesson, she was a little nervous—would she be able to flip like the girls on TV?

But the gym felt like a giant playground! There were foam pits, balance beams, bouncy floors, and trampolines. Aly jumped right in (literally!). With every cartwheel and handstand attempt, her love for gymnastics grew even more.

Practice, Practice, and More Practice!

Aly's heart was set on becoming the best gymnast she could be. She practiced every day after school—even on weekends! The more she practiced, the more fun it became. Sure, she fell off the beam a lot (and maybe landed on her head a few times), but Aly just laughed, stood up, and tried again.

She loved the feeling of flying through the air during a flip, and every time she nailed a new skill, she'd celebrate with a big smile. Soon, gymnastics became more than just a hobby—it became her favorite thing to do.

The "Gymnastics Bug" Bit Her for Good!

Before Aly knew it, gymnastics was in her heart forever. She loved the way it made her feel—strong, focused, and free. She even started to enjoy the hard parts, like practicing the same routine over and over.

She knew that every little wobble would make her better.

Her First Big Dream: Becoming an Olympian

Aly's love for gymnastics grew so big that she set a BIG goal for herself:

"I'm going to be in the Olympics one day!"

Even as a kid, she believed that if she worked hard enough, anything was possible. And she was right! Aly's journey began with love for the sport, but her determination, practice, and heart are what helped her achieve her dreams.

And that's how Aly Raisman fell in love with gymnastics—one flip, one fall, and one dream at a time! If you love something as much as Aly loved gymnastics, who knows? You might just become a champion too!

Aly Raisman's First Steps into Training

So, how did Aly go from flipping on the living room couch to becoming one of the best gymnasts in the world? Well, it all began when she took her first steps into serious training—a journey that would be filled with exciting flips, tricky challenges, and lots of fun along the way!

Signing Up for Gymnastics Classes

After Aly saw the 2004 Olympics on TV, she knew she had to start training if she wanted to become an amazing gymnast. So, her parents signed her up for a local gymnastics class. At first, Aly was just excited to bounce on the trampolines and jump into the foam pit (because who wouldn't love that?).

She wore her very first leotard—a sparkly outfit that made her feel like a real gymnast—and stepped into the gym with wide eyes. The gym was filled with colorful mats, uneven bars, balance beams, and big bouncy floors. To Aly, it looked like the coolest playground ever!

Learning the Basics: Cartwheels and Somersaults

In those early days, Aly's training focused on the simple but important moves. Her coaches taught her:

Cartwheels (with lots of wobbles at first!)

Forward and backward rolls (like somersaults, but fancier)

Handstands (which she sometimes fell out of and landed on her belly)

Even though these moves seemed simple, Aly's coaches told her something very important:

"If you master the basics, you'll be ready for the harder stuff later." And Aly listened! She practiced every day after school, making sure her cartwheels were smooth and her handstands were strong.

Making New Friends and Having Fun

Gymnastics wasn't just about hard work—it was also tons of fun! Aly loved meeting new friends at the gym. They cheered each other on and giggled when they made mistakes. Sometimes, Aly and her friends would try silly challenges, like seeing who could hold a handstand the longest or who could do the most cartwheels in a row.

Even when the training got tough, Aly never gave up—she always found ways to make it fun. After all, falling off the balance beam wasn't a failure if you could laugh and try again!

Practicing Balance on the Beam

The balance beam became one of Aly's favorite (but trickiest) events. At first, she kept falling off—left, right, and center! But her coach told her:

"The key is to keep your eyes forward and your arms steady."

Aly practiced walking on the beam again and again. Some days, she felt frustrated, but every time she fell, she got right back up. With each attempt, she felt more confident. Little by little, she learned how to leap and spin on the narrow beam without falling.

Training Routine Becomes a Habit

As Aly trained more and more, gymnastics became part of her daily life. On school days, she'd finish her homework quickly so she could head to the gym. Her afternoons were filled with flips, jumps, and stretching exercises. Even on weekends, Aly was in the gym, working on her routines.

Her parents helped her stay on track by making sure she ate healthy snacks (like fruits and peanut butter sandwiches) and got plenty of sleep. They also encouraged her by saying:

"It's not about being perfect—it's about getting better every day."

Learning Discipline and Focus

Gymnastics training wasn't always easy, and Aly had to learn two very important things:

Discipline: This means working hard even when you don't feel like it.

Focus: Staying calm and paying attention, even when things get tough.

Sometimes Aly felt tired after a long day of school, but she knew that every practice made her stronger. She told herself:

"One step at a time, one skill at a time."

Even if her flips weren't perfect yet, her coaches reminded her that progress takes time. They'd say:

"A champion isn't made in a day—it's made in the little things you do every day."

Her First Small Competitions

After months of hard work, Aly entered her first small gymnastics competition. She was nervous and excited—her heart was beating fast, and her hands felt a little sweaty. But when her name was called, Aly stepped onto the mat with a big smile.

She performed her routine the best she could. Was it perfect? Nope! But she didn't mind. Her parents cheered loudly, and her coach gave her a high-five at the end. Aly knew that winning wasn't the goal—the goal was to have fun and keep improving.

The Spark Grows Even Brighter

After that first competition, Aly felt even more in love with gymnastics. She knew that she wanted to train harder and go further. Each day at the gym became an adventure:

How many flips can I do today?
Can I make my balance beam routine even better?
What new move can I try next?
She was hooked! With every step forward, Aly's dream of becoming an Olympic gymnast felt a little closer. She knew that it would take years of hard work, but Aly was ready for the challenge.

And So Her Journey Began…

Aly's first steps into training were just the beginning of an amazing adventure. She fell, she laughed, and she got back up—again and again. Little did she know that all those cartwheels, flips, and fun moments with her friends would one day lead her to the biggest stage in the world: the Olympic Games!

And just like Aly, if you follow your heart, work hard, and never give up, you can achieve anything you dream of, too!

What do you think? Ready to start practicing some handstands now? Just remember: Have fun and keep flipping!

CHAPTER 3: Dreaming of the Olympics

Aly's Biggest Dream: Competing for Team USA

From the very beginning, Aly Raisman didn't just dream of doing cartwheels and backflips—her heart was set on something bigger. She wanted to compete at the Olympics for Team USA, wearing the red, white, and blue with pride. But getting there would take more than just love for the sport. It would take years of hard work, sacrifices, and determination.

A Big Dream Sparks in a Little Girl

After watching the gymnasts in the 2004 Olympics on TV, Aly knew exactly what she wanted:

"I want to be one of those girls, standing on the podium, with a gold medal around my neck!"

She imagined herself in the biggest arenas, performing in front of the whole world. But more than anything, she wanted to represent Team USA. Competing for her country was the biggest honor Aly could dream of. She loved the idea of being part of a team, working together to achieve greatness.

Training Harder Than Ever

When Aly decided she wanted to compete for Team USA, her training kicked into overdrive. Gymnastics went from a fun activity to a serious commitment. While other kids might have been playing video games or hanging out with friends, Aly was in the gym, practicing routines for hours every day.

Her coaches told her:

"If you want to make it to the Olympics, you have to give it your all."

So Aly did exactly that. She woke up early, trained hard, and learned to balance school with hours of practice. Even when things got tough, Aly kept going, thinking about her dream of wearing a Team USA leotard one day.

Making Sacrifices Along the Way

Chasing a big dream means making some tough choices. Aly had to miss out on birthday parties, school events, and even vacations. But she didn't mind—she knew that every sacrifice brought her closer to her dream.

Some days were super exhausting, but Aly reminded herself, "The hard work will be worth it!"

When her muscles felt sore, she told herself, "Just one more routine, and I'll get stronger!"

Her parents and coaches always supported her, cheering her on with every little step she took toward her goal.

A Team Player at Heart

Aly didn't just want to win as an individual—she dreamed of being part of something bigger than herself. She loved the idea of competing with teammates who shared the same passion and goals. In gymnastics, being on a team means trusting each other, cheering each other on, and giving it your best for the whole group.

She told herself, "When I make it to Team USA, I'll be the best teammate I can be."

Her First Chance to Shine: Junior Competitions

Before Aly could compete at the Olympics, she had to prove herself in many smaller competitions. She started competing at the national level, going up against some of the best young gymnasts in the country. These competitions were important stepping stones on her way to the top.

At first, things didn't always go perfectly—Aly had her fair share of falls and mistakes. But every time she messed up, she learned something new and got a little bit better. She told herself, "One day, all this hard work will pay off."

Getting Closer to the Big Dream

After years of hard work, Aly finally started to catch the attention of Team USA coaches. They noticed how focused, determined, and hardworking she was. Aly didn't just have talent—she had heart.

She worked harder than ever, nailing difficult routines on the balance beam, floor exercise, and uneven bars. Aly was finally getting closer and closer to making her dream come true!

The Moment She Made Team USA

All those years of dedication finally paid off when Aly got the biggest news of her life:

"Aly, you've been selected to represent Team USA!" Aly couldn't believe it—her dream had come true! She felt proud, excited, and a little nervous all at once. But most of all, she felt grateful. All those long hours in the gym, all the sacrifices, and all the falls she had endured were worth it.

When Aly put on her Team USA leotard for the first time, it was a magical moment. She looked in the mirror and smiled. "This is it," she thought. "I made it."

Marching with Team USA at the Olympics

Walking into the Olympic arena for the first time, with Team USA by her side, was a moment Aly would never forget. The stadium was filled with thousands of cheering fans, and she knew that millions more were watching from home. As she marched with her teammates, Aly felt so proud to represent her country.

She whispered to herself, "This is what I've been dreaming of all along."

Aly was ready to give her best performance ever—not just for herself, but for her team, her family, and everyone cheering her on from home.

A Dream That Came True, One Flip at a Time

Aly Raisman's biggest dream—competing for Team USA—came true because she believed in herself and never gave up. Even when things got hard, Aly kept going, knowing that every little step brought her closer to the stars. And the best part? She proved that with hard work, passion, and a little bit of courage, any dream is possible.

Practice, Practice, and More Practice!

If there's one thing Aly Raisman learned on her way to becoming a champion, it's that practice makes progress! Aly didn't just wake up one day knowing how to do flips, handstands, and cartwheels perfectly. It took hours and hours of practice every single day.

The Gym Becomes Her Second Home

When Aly decided she wanted to compete at the highest level, the gym became her happy place. She practiced her routines six days a week, spending hours working on each skill until it was just right. Some days, she spent extra time trying the same flip over and over. And if she didn't get it right the first time, she simply smiled and said, "Let's try it again!"

Morning, afternoon, or evening, Aly was always ready to practice.

Strength training, stretching, and balance work were all part of her routine.

Even when she was tired, Aly knew that every small effort added up to something big.

"Oops! Try Again!" Moments

Not every practice went perfectly. Sometimes Aly would slip off the balance beam or land on her back instead of her feet. But she didn't let those mistakes stop her. Instead, Aly treated every "oops" moment as a chance to get better.

Her coach would say, "Aly, every fall is just one step closer to mastering it." And Aly believed it. Each time she messed up, she jumped back up, dusted herself off, and tried again with a smile.

Building Strength and Confidence

Gymnastics isn't just about being flexible; it takes a lot of strength and focus. Aly worked hard to build her muscles and learn new routines. She lifted weights, ran, and did exercises to make sure she was strong enough to handle tough flips and jumps.

She also practiced visualizing her routines—imagining herself doing every movement perfectly in her mind. This helped her feel more confident when she was out on the competition floor. "I see it in my head, now I just need to make it happen!" Aly would say to herself.

The Fun Side of Practice

Even though practicing was hard work, Aly found ways to make it fun!

She would challenge herself by setting small goals, like doing five perfect cartwheels in a row.

Joking with her teammates between routines made long hours at the gym more enjoyable.

Aly even made up fun little songs in her head to help her remember routines!

She learned that if you enjoy the process, even hard work can feel like play.

Practicing Outside the Gym

Aly didn't stop practicing just because she wasn't at the gym!

She would stretch at home while watching TV.

Aly practiced her balance by standing on one foot while brushing her teeth.

And whenever she was walking, she would imagine herself doing perfect landings. "Stick the landing!" she'd think as she hopped over cracks in the sidewalk.

Patience Pays Off

Sometimes, it took weeks or even months for Aly to master a new skill. At times, she would get frustrated, thinking, "Why can't I get this right?" But Aly reminded herself: Big things take time. She knew that every hour of practice was bringing her closer to her dream.

With patience and determination, Aly found that the skills she thought were impossible at first became easy with time. And every time she finally nailed a new move, it felt like winning a gold medal all over again! "Yes! I did it!" she'd cheer, clapping her hands in excitement.

The Secret to Success

Aly learned that the key to becoming great at anything—whether it's gymnastics, drawing, or playing the piano—is practice, practice, and more practice! She would tell herself, "The more I practice, the closer I get to my dream." And that's exactly what happened.

So if you have something you want to be really good at, just remember Aly's story. Keep practicing, have fun with it, and never give up—because one day, you'll surprise yourself with how far you've come!

CHAPTER 4: The Road to the Big Stage

First Competitions and Medals

Once Aly Raisman had practiced for hours and hours in the gym, it was time for her to take a big leap and try her skills in competitions. This was where all her hard work would pay off!

Stepping onto the Competition Floor

Aly was both excited and nervous for her first competitions. She had watched so many amazing gymnasts compete on TV, and now it was her turn to step onto the big stage. "This is it!" she thought, her heart pounding in her chest.

Her first big competition was a local meet where gymnasts from nearby gyms came to show off their skills. Aly wore her shiny leotard, which sparkled under the bright lights. As she walked onto the floor, she felt like a star ready to shine.

The Thrill of Competing

When Aly started her routine, she focused on every movement. She performed a cartwheel, followed by a back handspring, and finished with a big smile. The audience cheered, and Aly felt like she was flying! Even though she made a few small mistakes, she was so proud of herself for having the courage to compete. She realized that it was about doing her best and having fun, no matter what the score would be.

A Sweet Surprise: Winning Her First Medal

At the end of the competition, it was time for the awards ceremony. Aly stood nervously with her teammates as they announced the winners. The announcer called out the names, and when she heard:

"And the gold medal goes to... Aly Raisman!"

Aly couldn't believe her ears! She jumped up and down, filled with excitement.

Aly rushed to the podium, where she was awarded her very first gold medal. It was shiny and heavy around her neck, and it felt like the most amazing treasure. She grinned from ear to ear, feeling proud and happy. "I did it! I really did it!" she thought, her heart soaring.

More Competitions and More Medals

After her first competition, Aly was ready for more! She entered many more meets, each time getting a little bit better and more confident. Each competition brought new challenges and opportunities to learn. She faced different routines on the balance beam, uneven bars, and floor.

Sometimes she placed first, and sometimes she didn't, but every time she learned something new.

Aly would come home and tell her family all about the competitions. She shared stories about falling off the beam, or how she nailed a tricky move, and most importantly, how she felt brave for trying.

The Journey to Bigger Competitions

As Aly continued to grow as a gymnast, she began to compete at the regional and national levels. With each competition, the stakes get higher, and so do her dreams! She practiced harder than ever, aiming to show off her best routines.

She competed against some of the best gymnasts in the country, and it was thrilling to be part of it all.

With every medal she earned, she felt herself getting closer to her goal of competing for Team USA.

Aly's Love for Winning, but More for the Journey

Winning medals was exciting, but for Aly, the real treasure was the joy of gymnastics. She loved the friendships she made, the lessons she learned, and the fun she had along the way.

At the end of each competition, whether she won gold or silver, Aly always remembered to celebrate with her friends. They would share stories, laugh, and cheer each other on, knowing that every medal was a symbol of their hard work and teamwork.

A Foundation for Greatness

Those first competitions and medals were just the beginning for Aly Raisman. Each win fueled her dream to become a top gymnast. With each medal, she learned that it wasn't just about the shiny awards—it was about the journey, the friendships, and the love for the sport.

Aly learned to embrace the ups and downs of competing, and she carried that spirit with her as she continued to pursue her dreams. The world was about to see just how far her dedication and hard work would take her!

So, whether you're winning medals or just having fun, remember: every step counts, and every moment is a chance to shine!

Overcoming Challenges Along the Way

Aly Raisman's journey to becoming a champion gymnast was filled with excitement and joy, but it wasn't all easy. Just like every superhero faces challenges, Aly had to overcome many obstacles to reach her dreams. Let's dive into her story of bravery, resilience, and determination!

Facing Fears

Every gymnast has to face their fears, and Aly was no exception. When she first started learning new tricks, she sometimes felt scared. Imagine trying to flip in the air or do a handstand on a wobbly balance beam!

The First Backflip: One day, Aly was learning how to do a backflip. She looked at the mat below and thought, "What if I fall?" But with a deep breath, she remembered what her coach always said: "Fear is just a part of the journey!" So she tried, fell a few times, and finally landed it!

Aly learned that facing fears makes you stronger, and every time she overcame a scary moment, she felt prouder of herself.

The Tough Days

Not every day in the gym was filled with sunshine and rainbows. There were tough days when Aly felt tired, frustrated, and even sad. Sometimes, she didn't land her routines the way she wanted to.

The Tiring Practices: One day, after a long practice, Aly sat on the floor, feeling a bit defeated. She thought, "Will I ever get better?" But then, she remembered the joy of gymnastics and the feeling of winning her first medal.

She realized that tough days were just a part of growing. So, she took a break, chatted with her teammates, and when she returned to practice, she felt refreshed and ready to try again.

Injuries Happen

As a gymnast, Aly sometimes faced injuries. Ouch! Falling or landing wrong can happen when you're flipping through the air. One time, Aly sprained her ankle during a practice session.

Learning to Rest: This was a tough moment for Aly. She loved being in the gym and didn't want to miss any practices. But her coach reminded her, "Rest is part of training too!" Aly learned that taking care of her body was essential to getting back to her best.

While she rested, Aly took the opportunity to learn more about gymnastics through videos and books. She stayed connected with her friends, cheering them on, which helped her feel less lonely during her recovery.

Balancing School and Gymnastics

As Aly's gymnastics career began to take off, she had to find a way to balance her schoolwork and training.

It wasn't easy! With so many practices and competitions, Aly had to be super organized.

Time Management Skills: She learned to plan her schedule carefully. Sometimes she would study in the car on the way to practice or do her homework right after school. It was all about staying focused and being responsible.

Aly's determination to succeed in both school and gymnastics taught her valuable lessons about time management and prioritizing what matters most.

Staying Positive

Aly knew that staying positive was essential, especially during challenging times. Whenever she faced difficulties, she reminded herself to keep a positive attitude.

The Power of Positivity: She would say things like, "I can do this!" or "I'm getting better every day!" Aly also found encouragement from her teammates and family, who cheered her on no matter what.

She discovered that a positive mindset could help her overcome any obstacle. Even on days when things didn't go as planned, Aly focused on the fun side of gymnastics, making her journey a lot brighter!

Learning from Setbacks

Sometimes, competitions didn't go as well as Aly had hoped. There were moments when she didn't place as high as she wanted, and that was disappointing. But instead of letting it get her down, Aly learned to look at these moments as learning opportunities.

The Growth Mindset: After a tough competition, she would sit down with her coach and review her performance. "What can I do better next time?" they would discuss. This helped her identify areas for improvement and grow as a gymnast.

Aly understood that setbacks are just stepping stones to success. Every disappointment made her more determined to improve and come back stronger.

A Champion's Spirit

Through all the challenges Aly faced, she developed a champion's spirit. She learned to embrace the ups and downs of gymnastics, knowing that each challenge was part of her journey.

Inspiration to Others: Aly's story inspired many young gymnasts around the world. She showed them that it's okay to stumble, fall, and even cry sometimes, as long as you keep getting back up and trying again.

With her hard work, positivity, and resilience, Aly Raisman proved that challenges can lead to greatness. So, the next time you face a challenge, remember Aly's story. Embrace it, learn from it, and keep pushing forward, just like a true champion!

CHAPTER 5: The 2012 London Olympics

Aly's Amazing Moments in London

In 2012, Aly Raisman experienced one of the most exciting times of her life when she competed in the London Olympics! This was her chance to shine on the world stage, and she made sure to make every moment count. Let's relive some of her amazing moments during this unforgettable event!

The Thrill of the Opening Ceremony

Aly arrived in London full of excitement and a little bit of nervousness. The Opening Ceremony was a dazzling display of lights, music, and incredible performances. As Aly walked into the stadium with her Team USA teammates, she felt like a superstar. Waving the Flag: Wearing her red, white, and blue uniform, she waved the American flag proudly. The crowd roared, and Aly's heart raced with joy. She knew that she was part of something special—a chance to represent her country in front of the world!

The Team Competition

The gymnastics competition began, and Aly was ready to show everyone what she could do. She was part of the U.S. Women's Gymnastics Team, which included other incredible gymnasts like Gabby Douglas and McKayla Maroney.

Nailing the Routines: During the team competition, Aly gave it her all. She performed a stunning floor routine filled with twists and turns, and her balance beam routine was so steady it looked like she was walking on a tightrope! With every move, she felt like she was flying.

When it was time for the scores to be announced, the crowd held its breath. When they heard Team USA had won the gold medal, Aly jumped up and down with her teammates, cheering and hugging each other. It was a magical moment that they would never forget!

The Moment of a Lifetime: Individual Events

After the team competition, Aly prepared for her individual events. She had worked hard for this, and she wanted to shine. Her first individual event was the floor exercise.

Dancing with Passion: As the music played, Aly dazzled the audience with her beautiful dance moves and high-flying flips. The crowd cheered louder and louder with each skill she nailed. When she finished, she raised her arms in victory, and everyone went wild!

Later, she competed in the balance beam and uneven bars. Despite the pressure, she performed each routine with grace and confidence. After her performances, Aly felt like she was on top of the world, no matter what the judges would say.

Winning Her First Gold Medal

Finally, it was time for Aly's biggest moment—competing in the individual all-around final! This was where the best gymnasts in the world competed for the title of champion.

The Big Day: Aly woke up that day feeling a mix of excitement and nerves. She knew she had to bring her best game. With every routine, she showed off her skills: flying on the floor, balancing perfectly on the beam, and executing flawless dismounts.

When the scores came in, the moment she had dreamed of finally arrived! Aly Raisman was crowned the Olympic champion, winning the gold medal in the individual all-around competition. She couldn't believe it!

Celebrating with Team USA

After the excitement of winning the gold, Aly celebrated with her teammates. They took selfies, danced, and laughed together, knowing they had all worked hard to achieve their dreams.

The Medal Ceremony: When it was time for the medal ceremony, Aly stood on the podium, her heart racing as they placed the gold medal around her neck. The national anthem played, and tears filled her eyes. She felt proud and grateful for everything she had accomplished.

Inspiring Young Gymnasts

Aly's amazing moments in London not only fulfilled her dreams but also inspired countless young gymnasts around the world. She showed them that with hard work, dedication, and belief in themselves, they could achieve anything.

A Role Model: After the Olympics, Aly became a role model for many kids who looked up to her. She encouraged them to chase their dreams, just like she did, proving that dreams really can come true!

A Legacy of Greatness

Aly Raisman's incredible journey at the London Olympics is a reminder that every moment counts, and every effort is worth it. From the opening ceremony to the podium, she created memories that would last a lifetime.

Whether she was nailing routines or celebrating with her teammates, Aly showed the world that with passion and perseverance, you can reach for the stars and shine brightly!

Aly's amazing moments in London were just the beginning of her incredible story, one filled with challenges, triumphs, and inspiration for gymnasts everywhere!

Winning Her First Gold Medal!

Winning a gold medal is a moment every athlete dreams of, and for Aly Raisman, that dream became a reality at the 2012 London Olympics! This incredible achievement marked a significant milestone in her gymnastics journey, filled with excitement, hard work, and unforgettable emotions. Let's dive into the thrilling story of how Italy won her very first gold medal!

The Big Day Arrives

The day Aly had been training for had finally arrived: the individual all-around final! She woke up feeling a mix of excitement and nerves. This was her chance to show the world all her hard work and dedication.

Morning Rituals: As she prepared for the competition, Aly made sure to eat a healthy breakfast. She focused on positive thoughts, reminding herself of all the practices she had completed. She knew that she was ready to give it her all.

The Warm-Up

Arriving at the Olympic venue, Aly and her teammates were buzzing with energy. They went through their warm-up routines, stretching and practicing their skills. Focusing on the Goal: Aly took a moment to breathe deeply and visualize her routines. She imagined herself performing flawlessly on the balance beam, uneven bars, and floor exercise. This mental preparation helped her feel confident and ready to shine.

Aly's Stellar Performance

When it was finally Aly's turn to compete, she stepped onto the mat with determination. Her routines were a blend of beautiful artistry and incredible athleticism.
Nailing the Floor Routine: Aly began with her floor exercise, performing stunning flips and twists that left the crowd in awe. She landed each jump perfectly, and the energy in the arena was electric. The audience cheered loudly, and Aly felt like she was flying!
Mastering the Balance Beam: Next was the balance beam, a challenging event where gymnasts must perform on a narrow beam just a few inches wide. Aly's routine was mesmerizing. She executed difficult skills with grace and precision, sticking to every landing. She felt proud and strong, knowing she was giving it her best.
Finishing Strong on the Uneven Bars: Finally, Aly tackled the uneven bars. With a powerful swing and perfect technique, she soared through her routine, performing beautiful releases and a flawless dismount. The crowd erupted in cheers as she landed.

The Moment of Truth

After all the routines were complete, it was time for the judges to announce the scores. Aly and her teammates huddled together, hearts racing with anticipation.

The Scores Are In: When the scores were revealed, Aly couldn't believe her eyes. She had finished with the highest score! Aly Raisman was crowned the Olympic champion in the individual all-around! It was a dream come true!

Celebrating the Victory

The moment she won was filled with pure joy and excitement. Aly jumped up and down with her teammates, celebrating their hard work and achievements together.

The Joy of Winning: Aly hugged her coach and teammates, tears of happiness streaming down her face. She had worked so hard for this moment, and it felt incredible to see her dreams come true.

The Medal Ceremony

The day wouldn't be complete without the medal ceremony! Aly stood on the podium, her heart pounding with pride.

Wearing the Gold Medal: As the gold medal was placed around her neck, she felt an overwhelming rush of emotions. The national anthem played, and Aly beamed with pride as she listened, thinking of all the sacrifices she and her family had made.

A Role Model: At that moment, Aly knew she had become a role model for young gymnasts everywhere. She was living proof that with hard work, dedication, and belief in yourself, dreams could become a reality.

Inspiring Others

Aly's journey to winning her first gold medal inspired countless kids around the world. She showed them that even though the path might be challenging, every moment spent practicing and believing in oneself could lead to amazing accomplishments.

Encouraging Young Gymnasts: After the Olympics, Aly made it her mission to encourage young athletes to follow their dreams. She shared her story, reminding kids that winning is not just about the medals but also about the hard work, friendship, and joy of pursuing your passion.

A Lasting Legacy

Winning her first gold medal at the London Olympics was not just a personal victory for Aly Raisman; it was a moment that showcased her incredible talent and determination.

The Beginning of Greatness: This achievement marked the beginning of her legacy as one of the greatest gymnasts in history. Aly's gold medal became a symbol of hope and inspiration for generations to come, proving that with dedication and heart, anything is possible!

Aly Raisman's journey to winning her first gold medal is a story filled with courage, hard work, and a sprinkle of magic. She showed the world what it means to be a true champion, inspiring all of us to dream big and reach for the stars!

CHAPTER 6:. A Leader on and off the Mat

Becoming the Captain of Team USA

Aly Raisman's journey in gymnastics was filled with hard work, dedication, and incredible moments. One of the most exciting parts of her story was when she became the captain of Team USA. This wasn't just about being a leader; it was about inspiring her teammates and showing the world what true teamwork means. Let's explore how Aly earned this special role and what it meant to her!

The Path to Leadership

Aly had always been a strong and passionate gymnast. She worked hard during her training sessions and pushed herself to be the best she could be. As she competed in various national and international competitions, her talent started to shine.

Gaining Experience: Over the years, Aly participated in many competitions, including the World Championships and the Olympics. With each event, she learned more about what it takes to be a champion, not just in skills but also in spirit and determination.

Earning the Trust of Teammates

As Aly continued to grow as a gymnast, she naturally developed into a leader. She encouraged her teammates, celebrated their successes, and supported them during tough times.

Being a Good Friend: Aly believed that being a captain meant being there for her teammates. She would always listen when they needed someone to talk to and cheer them on during practices. Her positive attitude made everyone feel confident and strong.

The Moment She Became Captain

In 2016, just before the Rio Olympics, Aly was named the captain of Team USA! This was an incredible honor and a huge responsibility.

Excitement and Responsibility: When Aly found out she would be leading her team, she was filled with excitement. She knew this was a special opportunity to guide her teammates through one of the most important competitions of their lives.

Leading by Example

As captain, Aly led by example. She showed her teammates the importance of hard work, determination, and sportsmanship.

Training Together: During training, Aly encouraged everyone to give their best effort. She reminded them that every practice was a chance to improve. If anyone was feeling down or frustrated, Aly was there to lift their spirits and help them focus on their goals.

Motivating the Team at the Olympics

When it was time for the Rio Olympics, Aly was ready to take on the role of captain. She was not just focused on her own performances; she wanted to ensure her entire team succeeded.

Building Team Spirit: Aly organized team huddles before competitions where everyone shared their thoughts and encouraged each other. She believed that teamwork made them stronger, and together they could achieve amazing things.

Facing Challenges Together

As captain, Aly also faced challenges. There were tough moments when things didn't go as planned, but she always reminded her teammates to stay positive and focused.

Overcoming Obstacles: After a tough practice or competition, Aly would gather everyone to talk about what they could learn from the experience. She emphasized the importance of resilience and how setbacks can help them grow.

Celebrating Success as a Team

When Team USA competed in the Rio Olympics, Aly's leadership shined. She cheered her teammates on and celebrated their achievements, whether big or small.

Winning Gold Together: When the U.S. Women's Gymnastics Team won the gold medal in the team competition, Aly couldn't contain her joy. She hugged her teammates, knowing that they had worked hard together to achieve this dream. It was a moment of triumph and unity.

Inspiring Future Generations

Aly's role as captain didn't just impact her teammates; it inspired countless young gymnasts around the world.

A Role Model for All: Through her leadership, Aly showed that being a captain is not just about winning but also about being a great friend, a motivator, and a supportive teammate. She encouraged young athletes to pursue their dreams and work together with kindness and respect.

A Legacy of Leadership

Becoming the captain of Team USA was one of the highlights of Aly Raisman's career. It taught her valuable lessons about teamwork, leadership, and the importance of supporting one another.

A Lasting Impact: Aly's journey from a young gymnast to captain inspired many kids to believe in themselves and their dreams. She proved that with hard work and a positive attitude, anyone can lead and make a difference.

Aly Raisman's story of becoming the captain of Team USA shows that true leadership comes from the heart. Her dedication, encouragement, and belief in her teammates made her an incredible captain and an inspiration to aspiring athletes everywhere!

What Makes Aly Raisman a Great Leader?

Aly Raisman is not just a remarkable gymnast; she is also an incredible leader. Throughout her career, she has shown that being a great leader is about more than just talent—it's about inspiring others, setting a good example, and showing kindness. Let's explore the qualities that make Aly such an amazing leader!

1. Inspiring Role Model

Aly leads by example, demonstrating what it means to work hard and stay dedicated.

Hard Work: She puts in countless hours of practice, showing her teammates that success comes from effort and perseverance.

Positive Attitude: Aly maintains a positive outlook, even during tough times, encouraging everyone to keep pushing forward.

2. Strong Communication Skills

Aly knows how to communicate effectively with her teammates, coaches, and fans.

Listening: She takes the time to listen to her teammates' concerns and ideas. This makes everyone feel valued and included.

Encouragement: Aly uses her words to lift others up. Whether it's a compliment or a motivating pep talk, she knows how to inspire confidence in others.

3. Team Spirit

Aly believes in the power of teamwork and camaraderie.

Building Relationships: She fosters strong bonds with her teammates, making everyone feel like part of a family.

Celebrating Success: Aly celebrates the achievements of her teammates, no matter how big or small. She understands that success is sweeter when shared.

4. Resilience and Determination

Aly demonstrates resilience in the face of challenges.

Overcoming Setbacks: When things don't go as planned, Aly doesn't give up. Instead, she learns from her experiences and encourages her teammates to do the same.

Encouraging Growth: She helps her teammates see challenges as opportunities for growth, reinforcing the idea that mistakes are part of the journey.

5. Compassion and Empathy

Aly shows compassion and empathy towards her teammates.

Being Supportive: When a teammate is feeling down or struggling, Aly is there to offer support and understanding.

Understanding Emotions: She recognizes that everyone has their ups and downs and provides a safe space for her teammates to express their feelings.

6. Setting High Standards

Aly sets high standards for herself and encourages her teammates to strive for greatness.

Expecting Excellence: She pushes herself to excel and inspires others to do the same, creating a culture of excellence within the team.

Goal-Oriented: Aly helps her teammates set and achieve their goals, whether in training or competitions.

7. Leading with Integrity

Aly demonstrates integrity in everything she does.

Doing the Right Thing: She stands up for what is right and encourages her teammates to act with honesty and fairness.

Being Accountable: Aly takes responsibility for her actions and decisions, showing her teammates the importance of accountability.

8. Creating a Fun and Positive Environment

Aly knows that enjoying the journey is just as important as reaching the destination.

Bringing Joy: She often brings fun and laughter to practices, helping to lighten the mood and create a positive atmosphere.

Encouraging Balance: Aly promotes a healthy balance between work and play, reminding her teammates to enjoy gymnastics and have fun while pursuing their dreams.

A True Leader

Aly Raisman's qualities as a leader go beyond her gymnastics skills. Her ability to inspire, communicate, support, and build strong relationships makes her a remarkable role model for young athletes everywhere. She shows that being a great leader is not just about winning medals, but about lifting others up and making a positive impact in their lives. Through her actions, Aly continues to inspire the next generation of gymnasts to believe in themselves and to lead with kindness and determination.

CHAPTER 7: 2016 Rio Olympics: Shining Again!

More Medals and Proud Moments

Aly Raisman's journey in gymnastics is filled with not only incredible hard work but also a collection of medals and proud moments that showcase her talent and determination. Let's dive into the highlights of Aly's achievements and the joyous moments that made her a celebrated figure in the world of gymnastics!

Winning Medals: A Dream Come True

Aly started her journey as a young girl dreaming of becoming an Olympic champion. Through years of dedication, she worked hard to turn that dream into reality. Here are some of her most memorable medal wins:

1. The 2012 London Olympics

Team Gold Medal: At the 2012 London Olympics, Aly and her teammates competed fiercely, ultimately winning the gold medal in the team event. This was a huge moment, as Aly felt the excitement of standing on the podium with her friends while the national anthem played. It was a dream come true!

Individual Events: In addition to the team gold, Aly also shined in individual events. She won a bronze medal in the individual all-around, where gymnasts perform on all apparatuses, and a silver medal on the floor exercise. These accomplishments showcased her versatility and skill.

2. The 2016 Rio Olympics

Team Gold Medal Again: In Rio, Aly was back with her teammates, and they once again delivered an outstanding performance. They won the gold medal in the team event, making Aly a two-time Olympic champion! The joy of winning together was a moment she would cherish forever.

Individual Achievements: Aly also competed in the individual all-around and floor exercise, earning a bronze medal in the all-around competition. The support from her teammates and fans made this moment even more special.

Proud Moments Beyond Medals

Aly's journey is not just defined by medals but also by the proud moments she experienced along the way.

1. Being a Role Model

Inspiring Young Gymnasts: Aly has always believed in the importance of inspiring the next generation. After her successes, she made it a point to connect with young athletes, sharing her journey and encouraging them to follow their dreams. Many young gymnasts looked up to her as a role model, which made Aly feel proud of her impact.

2. Speaking Out for Change

Advocating for Athletes: Aly used her platform to speak out against abuse in sports, becoming a voice for change. Her courage to share her story and advocate for safer environments in gymnastics showed her strength as a leader. This bravery earned her respect and admiration from people all over the world.

3. The "Final Five" Team

A Historic Team: Aly was part of the "Final Five," the nickname given to the U.S. Women's Gymnastics Team at the 2016 Rio Olympics. Being part of this iconic team and working alongside other talented gymnasts like Simone Biles and Laurie Hernandez made Aly proud. They supported each other, shared laughter, and created unforgettable memories.

4. Celebrating with Family and Friends

Family Support: Aly has always emphasized the importance of her family's support throughout her journey. After each competition, whether she won a medal or not, celebrating with her family brought her immense joy and pride. They cheered for her through thick and thin, and that made her achievements even more special.

Reflection on Achievements

Aly Raisman's journey is filled with not just medals, but also proud moments that reflect her character and resilience. Each medal she earned represents years of dedication, but her legacy goes beyond that. Aly has inspired countless young gymnasts to dream big, work hard, and stand up for what they believe in.

Her journey teaches us that while winning medals is fantastic, the relationships we build, the impact we make, and the courage we show are what truly define greatness. Aly Raisman's story is a celebration of hard work, friendship, and making a difference—values that everyone can aspire to!

Aly Raisman's Unforgettable Performances

Aly Raisman's gymnastics career is filled with breathtaking performances that have left audiences in awe and solidified her legacy as one of the sport's greats. From her powerful routines to her incredible grace, Aly has had many unforgettable moments. Let's take a closer look at some of her standout performances that showcased her talent, hard work, and determination!

1. The 2012 London Olympics: A Moment of Glory
Team Competition

The Dramatic Final Rotation: At the 2012 London Olympics, Aly played a crucial role in the team competition. During the final rotation on the floor exercise, Aly performed a flawless routine that secured the gold medal for Team USA. Her confidence and energy lit up the arena, and her teammates rallied behind her as she delivered one of the best performances of her career.

Emotional Victory: After the routine, Aly fell to her knees in tears of joy, celebrating not just her win but the hard work and dedication of her entire team. This moment is etched in the hearts of gymnastics fans around the world.

All-Around Final

Competing for Individual Glory: In the all-around final, Aly faced tough competition from other top gymnasts. However, she delivered exceptional performances on each apparatus, particularly on the balance beam, where her poise and precision shone through. She earned a bronze medal, showcasing her versatility and determination.

2. The 2016 Rio Olympics: A Champion's Comeback

Team Competition

Leading the Final Five: At the 2016 Rio Olympics, Aly returned as a leader of the "Final Five." In the team competition, she performed with poise and skill, contributing to another gold medal victory for Team USA. Her calmness under pressure and ability to inspire her teammates made this performance unforgettable.

Balance Beam Routine

A Show of Strength: One of the standout moments of Aly's Rio experience was her balance beam routine. It was packed with challenging elements, and she executed them flawlessly. The crowd held its breath as she landed each skill, showcasing her incredible focus and determination.

3. Floor Exercise: A Crowd Favorite

Emotional Storytelling

2012 Floor Routine: Aly's floor exercise routine during the 2012 Olympics captivated audiences with its combination of athleticism and artistry. Her performance told a story, and she connected with the crowd through her expressive movements. The routine culminated in a powerful final pass that earned her a standing ovation.

2016 Floor Routine

An Epic Finale: Aly's floor routine in the 2016 Olympics was equally memorable. With a mix of dynamic tumbling passes and elegant choreography, she left a lasting impression. The audience was on its feet as she finished her routine with a stunning smile and perfect landing.

4. World Championships: Showcasing Consistency

2015 World Championships

Bringing Home Gold: At the 2015 World Championships in Glasgow, Aly proved her consistency as a top gymnast. Her performances across multiple events earned her a gold medal in the team competition. Aly's ability to stay calm and focused in front of a global audience solidified her status as a world-class gymnast.

5. National Championships: Proving Her Dominance

2015 U.S. National Championships

A Standout Performance: At the 2015 U.S. National Championships, Aly delivered a series of exceptional routines, especially on the floor and balance beam. Her performances were marked by technical precision and emotional intensity, earning her the title of national champion.

6. The Power of Presence

Impact Beyond the Mat

A Role Model in Performance: Aly's performances were not just about the routines; they were about her presence. Her confidence, sportsmanship, and ability to connect with the audience made every competition a memorable event. She inspired countless young gymnasts to believe in themselves and strive for greatness.

A Legacy of Unforgettable Moments

Aly Raisman's unforgettable performances have left an indelible mark on the world of gymnastics. Her dedication, talent, and emotional connection to the sport have made her a beloved figure among fans and aspiring gymnasts alike. Each performance tells a story of hard work and passion, reminding us all that with determination and a love for what you do, you can achieve great things. Aly's legacy will inspire generations to come!

CHAPTER 8: The Power of Teamwork

How Aly and Her Teammates Supported Each Other

Aly Raisman's journey as a gymnast has been marked not only by her incredible performances but also by the strong bonds she formed with her teammates. These relationships played a crucial role in her success and well-being throughout her gymnastics career. Let's explore how Aly and her teammates supported each other, creating a strong sense of camaraderie and friendship!

1. Building Strong Friendships

Training Together

Shared Experiences: Aly and her teammates spent countless hours training together at the gym, practicing routines, and perfecting their skills. These shared experiences created a bond among them, allowing them to understand each other's struggles and triumphs.

Cheering Each Other On: During practice sessions, they cheered for one another and celebrated even the smallest achievements. This positive atmosphere helped everyone feel motivated and supported.

Emotional Support

Being There for Each Other: Gymnastics can be tough, both physically and emotionally. When one of them faced challenges or setbacks, the others were always there to lend an ear or offer a comforting hug. Aly often talked about how important it was to have her teammates by her side, ready to lift her spirits when she needed it most.

2. Team Spirit at Competitions

Rallying Together

Pre-Competition Rituals: Before big competitions, Aly and her teammates would have fun rituals, like dancing, chanting, or just spending time together. These moments helped ease nerves and build excitement, reminding them they were in it together.

Supporting Each Other on the Floor: During competitions, the teammates would cheer for one another from the sidelines, offering encouragement and motivation. They would shout words of support as each gymnast took her turn, creating an electric atmosphere of teamwork.

Celebrating Successes Together

Shared Victories: After winning medals or completing routines, Aly and her teammates celebrated together. Whether it was a group hug, jumping for joy, or simply soaking in the moment, these celebrations highlighted their shared achievements and reinforced their bond. Acknowledging Individual Strengths: Each gymnast brought something unique to the team. Aly and her teammates recognized and appreciated each other's strengths, whether it was on the balance beam, floor exercise, or vault. This understanding made them stronger as a team.

3. Overcoming Challenges Together

Facing Adversity

Supporting Each Other Through Injuries: Injuries are a part of sports, and Aly and her teammates faced their fair share. When one of them was injured, the others rallied around her, offering encouragement and support. They would check in on each other and remind their injured teammate that she was still a valuable part of the team, regardless of whether she was competing.

Building Resilience: During tough training sessions or after a disappointing performance, the teammates would help each other stay positive. They would talk about their goals, remind each other of their hard work, and encourage one another to keep pushing forward.

Emotional Resilience

Supporting Each Other's Mental Health: Aly and her teammates recognized the importance of mental health in their sport. They talked openly about their feelings and anxieties, creating a safe space where everyone felt comfortable expressing themselves. This mutual support helped them cope with the pressures of competition.

4. Celebrating Each Other's Achievements

Team Success

United in Victory: Aly and her teammates always emphasized that their successes were collective. When Team USA won gold medals, they celebrated together as a unit, understanding that each member played a vital role in their achievements.

Highlighting Individual Achievements: While they celebrated team victories, they also made sure to recognize individual accomplishments. If one gymnast earned a medal or delivered a standout performance, the others were quick to congratulate and applaud her efforts.

Creating Lasting Memories

Bonding Beyond Gymnastics: The friendships formed during their training and competitions led to lifelong memories. Whether it was sharing meals, going on trips, or just hanging out, these moments strengthened their relationships and created a sense of family within the team.

The Power of Teamwork and Friendship

Aly Raisman's journey in gymnastics is a testament to the power of teamwork and friendship. The support she and her teammates offered one another went beyond the gym; it created a strong foundation of trust and encouragement that fueled their success. Their shared experiences, emotional support, and celebrations of one another's achievements are reminders that true strength lies not only in individual talent but also in the bonds we create with others. Together, they showed the world what it means to be a united team, making their journey in gymnastics even more special!

Why Teamwork is So Important

Teamwork is a vital part of many activities and sports, including gymnastics. When people work together, they can achieve great things! Here's why teamwork is so important, especially in a team sport like gymnastics.

1. Achieving Common Goals

Working Towards Success Together: Teamwork helps everyone in the group focus on the same goals. In gymnastics, athletes train to win competitions, and when they work together, they can motivate and support each other to reach those goals.

Shared Victories: When a team wins a competition, it's a shared victory. Everyone feels a sense of pride and accomplishment, knowing that their efforts contributed to the team's success.

2. Building Strong Relationships

Friendships and Bonds: Teamwork creates strong friendships. Athletes who train and compete together often become close friends, supporting each other through challenges and celebrating successes together.

Trust and Communication: Working as a team helps build trust. Gymnasts learn to communicate effectively, share their feelings, and rely on one another during training and competitions.

3. Developing Skills Together

Learning from Each Other: Teamwork allows athletes to learn from one another. Experienced gymnasts can share tips and techniques with newer teammates, helping everyone improve their skills.

Encouraging Growth: When teammates support each other, they help each other grow. Constructive feedback and encouragement can boost confidence and lead to better performances.

4. Boosting Motivation and Morale

Staying Positive: In a team, it's easier to stay motivated. When one member is feeling down or discouraged, the others can lift their spirits with encouragement and support.

Creating a Fun Environment: Teamwork makes training and competitions more enjoyable! Working together creates a fun and energetic atmosphere where everyone can thrive.

5. Overcoming Challenges Together

Facing Adversity as a Team: When challenges arise, whether it's a tough competition or a setback, teamwork helps everyone handle the situation. Working together means sharing the load and finding solutions as a group.

Resilience and Strength: Teamwork fosters resilience. When teammates support each other during tough times, they can bounce back stronger and more determined.

6. Enhancing Performance

Perfecting Routines: In gymnastics, teamwork allows gymnasts to practice routines together, providing feedback that can enhance each performance. This collaboration can lead to better execution and higher scores.

Team Dynamics: Strong teamwork creates a positive dynamic, making each individual feel valued and encouraged. This positive environment can lead to outstanding performances.

7. Lifelong Skills

Important Life Lessons: Teamwork teaches valuable life skills, such as communication, problem-solving, and collaboration. These skills are useful not just in sports but in school, work, and everyday life.

Building Character: Working as a team helps individuals develop character traits like respect, responsibility, and empathy, which are essential for building strong relationships in all areas of life.

The Power of Teamwork

Teamwork is the heart of success in many sports, including gymnastics. It fosters friendships, boosts motivation, and helps individuals grow both as athletes and as people. When athletes come together as a team, they create a powerful bond that allows them to achieve amazing things and enjoy the journey along the way. Remember, together everyone achieves more!

CHAPTER 9: Standing Up for What's Right

Aly's Courage to Speak Out

Aly Raisman is not just an incredible gymnast; she is also a courageous advocate for change. Throughout her career, she has shown remarkable bravery by using her voice to speak out on important issues. Let's explore how Aly's courage to speak out has made a difference in the lives of many!

1. Standing Up Against Abuse

A Voice for Victims

Sharing Her Story: Aly courageously shared her own experiences of abuse in gymnastics, becoming a powerful voice for many who had suffered in silence. By speaking out, she shed light on a serious issue that had affected countless athletes, encouraging others to come forward.

Breaking the Silence: Aly's decision to speak out helped break the silence surrounding abuse in sports. She showed that it is essential to talk about uncomfortable topics to create a safer environment for everyone.

Empowering Others

Inspiring Others to Speak Up: Aly's bravery inspired many other athletes to share their stories. She showed them that they were not alone and that their voices mattered. This ripple effect led to a larger movement advocating for change and accountability in gymnastics and other sports.

2. Advocating for Change in Gymnastics

Demanding Accountability

Pushing for Investigations: Aly was a key figure in advocating for investigations into the culture of abuse in gymnastics. She worked tirelessly to ensure that those responsible were held accountable for their actions, aiming to create a safer environment for young athletes.

Testifying Before Congress: Aly took her fight to the next level by testifying before Congress, urging lawmakers to implement changes that would protect athletes from abuse. This act of courage showcased her determination to bring about real change.

Working with Organizations

Partnering with Advocacy Groups: Aly has collaborated with various organizations that focus on athlete safety and rights. Through these partnerships, she has worked to create programs and policies that prioritize the well-being of athletes in sports.

3. Promoting Mental Health Awareness

Speaking About Mental Health

Normalizing the Conversation: Aly has been open about the mental health challenges athletes face, helping to destigmatize the topic. She encourages young athletes to prioritize their mental health and seek help when needed.

Encouraging Self-Care: By sharing her experiences, Aly reminds others that it's okay to take a break, ask for help, and focus on self-care. She emphasizes that mental well-being is just as important as physical health.

4. Using Her Platform for Good

Social Media Advocacy

Raising Awareness: Aly uses her social media platforms to raise awareness about important issues affecting athletes and the broader community. She shares resources, stories, and information to help educate others.

Encouraging Positive Change: Through her posts, Aly encourages her followers to stand up for what is right, advocate for change, and support one another. She inspires many to take action in their communities.

Speaking Engagements

Sharing Her Message: Aly often speaks at events, schools, and organizations, sharing her story and advocating for change. Her speeches are powerful and moving, inspiring audiences to reflect on the importance of courage and standing up for justice.

5. Leaving a Lasting Impact

Creating a Safer Future

Building a Culture of Safety: Aly's courage to speak out has contributed to creating a culture of safety in gymnastics and beyond. Her efforts are paving the way for future generations of athletes to feel safe and supported in their sports.

Inspiring Change in Sports: By addressing important issues, Aly has sparked conversations about athlete safety and well-being, encouraging changes not only in gymnastics but also in other sports.

A True Champion

Aly Raisman's courage to speak out has made her a true champion both in and out of the gymnastics arena. Her bravery in sharing her story and advocating for change has inspired countless others to find their voices. Aly teaches us that it's essential to stand up for what is right, support one another, and work together to create a safer and more inclusive environment for everyone. Her legacy will continue to inspire future generations to speak out, advocate for change, and make a difference!

Making a Difference Beyond Gymnastics

Aly Raisman's impact extends far beyond the world of gymnastics. While she is celebrated for her incredible athletic achievements, she has also dedicated her life to making a positive difference in the world. Let's explore how Aly is making waves in various areas and inspiring others along the way!

1. Advocating for Athlete Safety

Creating Change in Sports Organizations

Pushing for Policy Reforms: Aly's advocacy for athlete safety has led to significant changes in policies within gymnastics and other sports organizations. She has worked tirelessly to ensure that safety protocols are in place to protect athletes from abuse and harm.

Collaborating with Leaders: By collaborating with leaders in sports, Aly is helping to create a culture of accountability and transparency, making sports safer for everyone involved.

Empowering Young Athletes

Inspiring Courage: Aly encourages young athletes to speak up about their experiences and to advocate for themselves. She emphasizes that everyone has the right to feel safe and respected in their sport, empowering the next generation to stand up for what is right.

2. Promoting Mental Health Awareness

Destigmatizing Mental Health Issues

Sharing Her Journey: Aly openly discusses her mental health challenges, helping to destigmatize the topic and encouraging others to seek help when they need it. She emphasizes that mental health is just as important as physical health.

Encouraging Open Conversations: By normalizing conversations about mental health, Aly creates a safe space for athletes and others to talk about their struggles, fostering a supportive community.

Creating Supportive Resources

Partnering with Organizations: Aly collaborates with mental health organizations to provide resources and support for athletes and their families. She believes that mental health education is crucial for creating a healthy environment for young athletes.

3. Empowering Women and Girls

Championing Gender Equality

Advocating for Equal Opportunities: Aly is a vocal advocate for gender equality in sports. She believes that all athletes, regardless of gender, should have equal opportunities to compete, succeed, and be treated with respect.

Inspiring Future Leaders: By using her platform to promote women's empowerment, Aly inspires young girls to pursue their dreams, whether in sports or any other field. She encourages them to believe in themselves and strive for greatness.

Supporting Women's Rights

Raising Awareness: Aly raises awareness about issues affecting women and girls, such as body positivity, self-esteem, and the importance of standing up against discrimination. She uses her voice to advocate for women's rights and inspire change.

4. Giving Back to the Community

Engaging in Philanthropy

Supporting Charitable Causes: Aly is actively involved in various charitable organizations and initiatives. She donates her time and resources to help those in need, making a difference in her community and beyond.

Promoting Health and Wellness: Through her charitable work, Aly promotes health and wellness initiatives, encouraging people to lead active and healthy lives. She understands the importance of physical and mental well-being.

Visiting Schools and Communities

Inspiring Young Minds: Aly frequently visits schools and community events to share her story and inspire young people. She encourages them to pursue their passions, work hard, and believe in themselves, regardless of the obstacles they may face.

5. Raising Awareness on Important Issues

Using Her Platform Wisely

Speaking Out on Social Issues: Aly uses her social media platforms to raise awareness about various social issues, including abuse, mental health, and equality. She believes in the power of social media to inspire change and spread important messages.

Encouraging Civic Engagement: Aly encourages her followers to get involved in their communities and be active citizens. She believes that everyone can make a difference, no matter how small their actions may seem.

A Role Model for All

Aly Raisman's impact goes beyond gymnastics; she is a true champion for change. Her courage, advocacy, and dedication to making a difference in the world inspire countless individuals to stand up for what is right and to work towards a better future. Aly teaches us that we all have the power to make a difference, whether through our actions, words, or support for one another. By using her voice for good, Aly continues to inspire and uplift others, leaving a lasting legacy of hope, strength, and courage for future generations.

CHAPTER 10: A Life of Inspiration

What Aly Raisman is Doing Today

Aly Raisman, the incredible gymnast and advocate, continues to inspire people around the world long after her Olympic glory. Let's take a look at what she is doing today!

1. Continuing Her Advocacy Work

Fighting for Athlete Safety

Advocating for Change: Aly is still a strong voice for athlete safety and well-being. She continues to work with various organizations and leaders in sports to create policies that protect young athletes from abuse.

Speaking Engagements: Aly frequently speaks at events and conferences, sharing her story and advocating for changes that promote a safer environment in sports. Her powerful messages resonate with athletes, coaches, and parents alike.

Promoting Mental Health Awareness

Spreading the Message: Aly is committed to raising awareness about mental health issues, especially in the sports community. She emphasizes the importance of mental well-being and encourages athletes to prioritize their mental health alongside their physical training.

Collaborating with Organizations: Aly partners with mental health organizations to provide resources and support for athletes struggling with mental health challenges, helping to destigmatize the topic.

2. Engaging with Fans and the Community

Social Media Presence

Inspiring Others: Aly actively engages with her fans on social media, sharing updates about her life, advocacy work, and personal insights. Her posts often include messages of positivity, encouragement, and empowerment.

Creating Fun Content: Aly shares fun and relatable content, from workouts to daily life, connecting with her audience and showing that she is just like them, while also being a champion.

School Visits and Community Events

Inspiring Young Athletes: Aly visits schools and community events to share her journey and inspire the next generation of athletes. Her speeches encourage kids to dream big, work hard, and believe in themselves.

Promoting Healthy Living: Through these visits, Aly promotes the importance of physical activity, teamwork, and resilience, teaching young people valuable life lessons.

3. Staying Active in Sports

Fitness and Training

Staying Fit: While Aly may not compete in gymnastics anymore, she remains dedicated to fitness. She enjoys various forms of exercise, including workouts that focus on strength, flexibility, and overall health.

Participating in Events: Aly participates in fitness events and challenges, showcasing her athleticism and encouraging others to stay active.

Engaging in Sports Commentary

Commentating on Gymnastics: Aly has made guest appearances as a commentator during gymnastics events, sharing her expert insights and experiences with viewers. Her knowledge of the sport adds depth to the coverage and inspires fans.

4. Writing and Creating

Authoring Books

Inspiring Young Readers: Aly has authored books, including her memoirs and children's books, where she shares her experiences and lessons learned. These books inspire young readers to pursue their dreams and overcome challenges.

Creating Educational Content: Aly often collaborates with organizations to create educational materials that promote athlete safety and well-being, making a positive impact in the community.

Building a Brand

Developing Merchandise: Aly is involved in creating merchandise, including clothing and accessories, that reflects her brand and advocacy work. She uses her platform to promote messages of empowerment and resilience.

5. Leading a Balanced Life

Focusing on Personal Growth

Prioritizing Mental Well-Being: Aly emphasizes the importance of mental health and self-care in her life. She shares tips and strategies for managing stress and maintaining a healthy work-life balance.

Pursuing New Interests: Aly explores various hobbies and interests outside of gymnastics, including traveling, cooking, and spending time with family and friends. She believes in the importance of enjoying life and finding joy in everyday moments.

Advocating for Positive Change

Supporting Charitable Causes: Aly is involved in various charitable organizations and initiatives, using her platform to raise funds and awareness for causes close to her heart, such as mental health and youth empowerment.

A Lasting Impact

Today, Aly Raisman continues to shine brightly as a champion both in and out of the gymnastics arena. Her advocacy work, community engagement, and commitment to mental health awareness demonstrate her dedication to making a difference. Aly serves as a role model for young athletes and individuals everywhere, showing that with courage, determination, and a willingness to speak out, anyone can create positive change in the world.

How Aly Raisman Inspires Kids to Follow Their Dreams

Aly Raisman, a world-renowned gymnast and advocate, is not just an Olympic champion; she is a source of inspiration for children everywhere. Her journey from a young girl dreaming of greatness to a celebrated athlete shows kids that with hard work, dedication, and belief in themselves, they can achieve anything. Here are some of the ways Aly inspires kids to follow their dreams:

1. Sharing Her Personal Story

Relatable Journey

From a Dreamer to a Champion: Aly often shares her story of starting gymnastics at a young age and working hard to overcome obstacles. She talks about her early dreams of being an Olympian, making it relatable for kids who have their own aspirations.

Facing Challenges: Aly openly discusses the challenges she faced, including injuries and setbacks. By sharing these experiences, she shows kids that it's okay to stumble along the way and that persistence is key.

Encouraging Self-Belief

Believe in Yourself: Aly emphasizes the importance of believing in oneself. She encourages kids to trust their abilities and pursue their passions, no matter how big or small.

2. Promoting a Strong Work Ethic

Dedication to Training

Hard Work Pays Off: Aly often talks about the countless hours she spent training and perfecting her routines. She emphasizes that success doesn't come overnight and that dedication is essential for achieving goals.

Setting Goals: Aly encourages kids to set both short-term and long-term goals for themselves. She teaches them to break their dreams into smaller, achievable steps, making it easier to stay motivated.

Positive Attitude Toward Failure

Learning from Mistakes: Aly teaches kids that mistakes are a part of the journey. She shares stories of times she fell or made errors during competitions, reminding kids that every setback is an opportunity to learn and grow.

3. Empowering Through Advocacy

Championing Athlete Safety

Speaking Out: Aly uses her platform to advocate for athlete safety and mental health awareness. By standing up for what is right, she teaches kids the importance of using their voices to make a difference and to protect themselves and others.

Creating a Supportive Environment: Aly's work encourages children to speak out if they ever feel uncomfortable or unsafe. She inspires them to create a supportive community where everyone looks out for one another.

Promoting Mental Health Awareness

Prioritizing Well-Being: Aly stresses the importance of mental health, encouraging kids to take care of their minds as well as their bodies. She inspires them to seek help when they need it and to talk openly about their feelings.

4. Leading by Example

Being a Role Model

Demonstrating Kindness and Humility: Aly exemplifies kindness, humility, and generosity in her interactions with fans and fellow athletes. She shows kids that being a champion is not just about winning but also about being a good person.

Encouraging Teamwork: Aly highlights the importance of teamwork and supporting one another. She inspires kids to work together, celebrate each other's successes, and lift each other up during tough times.

Engaging with the Community

School Visits and Workshops: Aly frequently visits schools and community centers, sharing her experiences and encouraging children to pursue their dreams. Through fun workshops and motivational talks, she connects with kids and shows them that they can achieve greatness.

5. Embracing Creativity and Passion

Encouraging Individuality

Be True to Yourself: Aly inspires kids to embrace their unique talents and interests. She encourages them to explore various activities, whether it's sports, art, or music, reminding them that following their passions is what truly matters.

Finding Joy in the Journey: Aly teaches kids to find joy in the process of pursuing their dreams. She believes that passion and enjoyment make the journey worthwhile, no matter the outcome.

A Beacon of Inspiration

Aly Raisman's journey serves as a powerful reminder that dreams can come true with hard work, dedication, and a positive mindset. Through her advocacy, personal story, and commitment to inspiring the next generation, Aly empowers kids to follow their dreams and believe in themselves. She teaches them that while the road may have challenges, with perseverance and passion, they can achieve anything they set their minds to. Aly is not just a gymnast; she is a beacon of hope and inspiration for children everywhere.

CHAPTER 11: Words of Wisdom from Aly

Aly Raisman's Advice to Young Dreamers

Aly Raisman, the incredible gymnast and advocate, has valuable advice for young dreamers who aspire to achieve their goals, whether in sports, academics, or any other area of life. Here are some of her key pieces of advice that can inspire and guide kids on their journey to success:

1. Believe in Yourself

Self-Confidence is Key: Aly emphasizes the importance of believing in your own abilities. She encourages kids to trust themselves and have confidence in their skills, reminding them that self-belief is the first step toward achieving their dreams.

Embrace Your Uniqueness: Aly tells kids that everyone has unique talents and strengths. Instead of comparing themselves to others, they should focus on what makes them special and embrace their individuality.

2. Set Goals and Work Hard

Break It Down: Aly advises young dreamers to set both short-term and long-term goals. She encourages them to break their big dreams into smaller, achievable steps, making it easier to stay motivated and track progress.

Dedication and Commitment: She reminds kids that success requires hard work and dedication. Aly shares that training and practicing consistently is essential to achieving goals, even when it gets tough.

3. Learn from Failures

Mistakes are Opportunities: Aly teaches kids that everyone makes mistakes and that it's okay to fail. Instead of feeling discouraged, they should view failures as valuable learning experiences that help them grow and improve.

Keep Trying: She encourages young dreamers to persevere and keep trying, even when things don't go as planned. Resilience is a vital quality that can help them overcome challenges and reach their dreams.

4. Surround Yourself with Support

Build a Positive Team: Aly emphasizes the importance of having a support system, whether it's family, friends, coaches, or teammates. Surrounding themselves with positive, encouraging people can motivate them to work harder and achieve their goals.

Lift Each Other Up: She encourages kids to support one another and celebrate each other's successes. Teamwork and collaboration can make the journey even more enjoyable and rewarding.

5. Prioritize Mental Health

Take Care of Your Mind: Aly advocates for mental health awareness and encourages kids to prioritize their mental well-being. She advises them to talk about their feelings, seek help when needed, and practice self-care.

Balance is Important: Aly believes in the importance of finding a balance between pursuing dreams and enjoying life. She encourages kids to make time for fun, hobbies, and relaxation.

6. Speak Up and Be Brave

Use Your Voice: Aly inspires kids to speak up for themselves and others. She emphasizes that it's important to advocate for what is right and to stand up against negativity or unfair treatment.

Embrace Courage: She teaches young dreamers that being brave doesn't mean being fearless; it means taking action even when you feel scared. Courage can lead to incredible opportunities and positive change.

7. Enjoy the Journey

Find Joy in Every Moment: Aly reminds kids to enjoy the process of pursuing their dreams. It's not just about the end goal but also about the experiences, friendships, and lessons learned along the way.

Celebrate Small Wins: She encourages kids to celebrate their achievements, no matter how small. Recognizing progress can help maintain motivation and a positive outlook.

Dream Big and Shine Bright

Aly Raisman's advice to young dreamers is rooted in self-belief, hard work, resilience, and the importance of support and mental health. She inspires kids to pursue their passions fearlessly, reminding them that the journey toward their dreams can be just as rewarding as reaching the finish line. With Aly's wisdom as their guide, young dreamers can embrace their unique paths and shine brightly in all they do.

Test Your Knowledge About Aly Raisman!

What year did Aly Raisman first compete in the Olympics?

---

a) 2008
b) 2012
c) 2016

Which gymnastics event is Aly known for winning multiple medals in?

a) Floor Exercise
b) Balance Beam
c) All-Around

What role did Aly Raisman have on the U.S. gymnastics team during the 2016 Olympics?

a) Team member
b) Coach
c) Captain

How many Olympic gold medals has Aly Raisman won?

a) 1
b) 2
c) 3

What is the title of Aly's memoir?

a) "Fierce"
b) "Brave"
c) "Strong"

Which gymnastics team did Aly Raisman compete for during her career?

    a) The Magnificent Seven
    b) The Fierce Five
    c) The Final Five

What significant issue did Aly Raisman speak out about after her gymnastics career?

    a) Athlete safety
    b) Nutrition
    c) Travel expenses

In which state did Aly Raisman grow up?

    a) California
    b) New Jersey
    c) Massachusetts

What is Aly Raisman's full name?

    a) Alyson Rae Raisman
    b) Alyson Marie Raisman
    c) Alyson Anne Raisman

What is one of Aly's hobbies outside of gymnastics?

a) Painting
b) Cooking
c) Dancing

Answers:

b) 2012
a) Floor Exercise
c) Captain
b) 2
a) "Fierce"
c) The Final Five
a) Athlete safety
c) Massachusetts
a) Alyson Rae Raisman
c) Dancing

CONCLUSION

Aly Raisman is an American gymnast who has inspired millions with her dedication, talent, and courage. Born on May 25, 1994, in Needham, Massachusetts, Aly fell in love with gymnastics at a young age, inspired by her parents and the 1996

Olympic team. She began training seriously and quickly progressed through the ranks, showcasing her incredible skills and passion for the sport.

Early Career and First Olympics (2012)

Aly made her mark on the gymnastics world when she competed at the 2012 London Olympics as a member of the "Fierce Five." Her performances included outstanding routines on the floor exercise and balance beam, earning her gold medals in both events. Aly's incredible all-around performance led the U.S. team to a gold medal, and she became a household name.

Continued Success and Leadership (2016)

Aly returned to the Olympics in 2016, this time as the captain of the "Final Five" team. Her leadership and expertise guided her teammates to victory, where they collectively secured a gold medal in the team event and individual medals in various categories. Aly also won a bronze medal in the individual all-around competition.

Overcoming Challenges

Throughout her career, Aly faced numerous challenges, including injuries and the pressure of high-stakes competitions. However, her resilience and hard work helped her push through these difficulties, showcasing her determination and passion for gymnastics.

Advocacy and Impact

After retiring from gymnastics, Aly became an outspoken advocate for athlete safety and mental health. She bravely spoke out about the abuse she and other gymnasts faced, emphasizing the need for change in the sport. Aly's courage has inspired many young athletes to use their voices and advocate for their rights.

Legacy and Inspiration

Aly Raisman's journey is a testament to hard work, resilience, and the power of following one's dreams. She has not only achieved remarkable success in gymnastics but has also made a lasting impact on the sport and its community. Through her advocacy, she inspires young dreamers to believe in themselves, work hard, and stand up for what is right.

Aly Raisman continues to be a role model for children everywhere, proving that with dedication, passion, and courage, they can achieve their dreams, no matter the obstacles they face.

Glossary of Terms

Athlete: A person who competes in sports or physical activities. Athletes train hard to improve their skills and perform well in competitions.

Balance Beam: A narrow beam used in gymnastics where gymnasts perform routines. It's a challenging event that requires balance and precision.

Captain: The leader of a team. In gymnastics, the captain helps guide and support teammates during competitions.

Competition: An event where athletes compete against each other to see who performs the best. Gymnasts often participate in competitions to showcase their skills.

Dedication: A strong commitment to a goal or task. Aly Raisman showed dedication by practicing gymnastics for many hours every week.

Gold Medal: An award given to the first-place winner in a competition. Aly won gold medals at the Olympics for her outstanding performances.

Gymnastics: A sport that involves exercises, routines, and performances on different apparatus, like the floor, balance beam, and uneven bars.

Injury: Physical harm or damage to the body, often causing pain and requiring time to heal. Injuries can happen in sports and may affect an athlete's ability to compete.

Olympics: A major international sporting event held every four years, where athletes from around the world compete in various sports, including gymnastics.

Routine: A series of movements or exercises performed in gymnastics. Routines are choreographed and judged based on difficulty and execution.

Teamwork: Working together with others to achieve a common goal. Aly emphasized the importance of teamwork in gymnastics, as it helps support and uplift each other.

Advocacy: Supporting a cause or speaking up for what is right. Aly Raisman advocates for athlete safety and mental health awareness.

Resilience: The ability to bounce back from challenges and difficulties. Aly showed resilience by overcoming injuries and pressures in her gymnastics career.

Silver Medal: An award given to the second-place winner in a competition. Aly won silver medals in addition to her gold medals at the Olympics.

Training: The practice and preparation athletes do to improve their skills and physical abilities. Aly trained for many years to become an elite gymnast.

Floor Exercise: A gymnastics event performed on a mat, where gymnasts showcase their routines with tumbling and dance elements.

Advocate: A person who supports or speaks out for a cause. Aly Raisman is an advocate for athlete safety and mental health.

Fierce Five: The nickname for the U.S. gymnastics team that competed in the 2012 Olympics and won the gold medal.

Final Five: The nickname for the U.S. gymnastics team that competed in the 2016 Olympics, where Aly served as captain.

Leadership: The ability to guide and support a group. Aly displayed strong leadership skills as the captain of her gymnastics team.

Made in the USA
Monee, IL
27 March 2025

14756785R00059